D0232699

COLD
PASTORAL

ALSO BY REBECCA DUNHAM

The Flight Cage

The Miniature Room

Glass Armonica

COLD
PASTORAL

REBECCA DUNHAM

POEMS

MILKWEED EDITIONS

Published 2017 by Milkweed Editions
Printed in the United States of America
Cover design by Gretchen Achilles
Cover photo by Carrie Vonderhaar / Ocean Futures Society / National Geographic Creative
Author photo by Amanda Crim / Second Nature Photography
17 18 19 20 21   5 4 3 2 1
First Edition

Milkweed Editions, an independent nonprofit publisher, gratefully acknowledges sustaining support from the Jerome Foundation; the Lindquist & Vennum Foundation; the McKnight Foundation; the National Endowment for the Arts; the Target Foundation; and other generous contributions from foundations, corporations, and individuals. Also, this activity is made possible by the voters of Minnesota through a Minnesota State Arts Board Operating Support grant, thanks to a legislative appropriation from the arts and cultural heritage fund, and a grant from the Wells Fargo Foundation. For a full listing of Milkweed Editions supporters, please visit www.milkweed.org.

Library of Congress Cataloging-in-Publication Data

Names: Dunham, Rebecca, 1973- author.
Title: Cold pastoral : poems / Rebecca Dunham.
Description: Minneapolis : Milkweed Editions, 2017.
Identifiers: LCCN 2016029440 (print) | LCCN 2016037781 (ebook) | ISBN 9781571314789 (softcover) | ISBN 9781571319395 (e-book)
Subjects: | BISAC: POETRY / American / General.
Classification: LCC PS3604.U54 A6 2017 (print) | LCC PS3604.U54 (ebook) | DDC 811/.6--dc23
LC record available at https://lccn.loc.gov/2016029440

Milkweed Editions is committed to ecological stewardship. We strive to align our book production practices with this principle, and to reduce the impact of our operations in the environment. We are a member of the Green Press Initiative, a nonprofit coalition of publishers, manufacturers, and authors working to protect the world's endangered forests and conserve natural resources. *Cold Pastoral* was printed on acid-free 30% postconsumer-waste paper by Versa Press.

CONTENTS

Carry abroad the urgent need, the scene,

to photograph and to extend the voice,

to speak this meaning.

Voices to speak to us directly.

—MURIEL RUKEYSER,
"The Book of the Dead"

COLD
PASTORAL

MNEMOSYNE TO THE POET

For you, memory is but
an oil lamp to snuff, left to
smoke. Diademed by earth's
velvet mantle. So easy

for you to ignore: hadal
press of sea, the open
vein's plumes,
how they wheel like

a maelstrom up and down.
My sight spills through
waves of old, blown
glass. I am not permitted

to turn, pillow to cheek,
and wait for sleep to find me.
Am not permitted
to learn how not to look.

ELEGY, WIND-WHIPPED

May 23, 2011, Joplin, Missouri

1. REFUSE

Doll hair—brown yarn—
loops round a hickory's jagged
limb and she dances

the wind like a human body

clinched above
the gallows. See—your own

eyes stitched open as hers—
there is no difference, batting
or flesh, still you will
hang, emptied by my breath.

She could be dead. Easily

she could be your daughter.

2. HAMPSHIRE TERRACE

Search and mark with a spray-
painted *X*. Nothing left
to salvage. You do not like

to say it, but you need
the dogs. No tools you possess
can help you find silence.

We're always hopeful but we briefed
the guys to plan for the worst.

Crowbar, chainsaw, chisel
you dig, hail beating.
In time, you think,
                please let me be in time.

3. LIST

Tilt, slant, heel—a careening, a leaning, to one side. Incline. To please, to like, to desire. To cut away in narrow strips, stave and plank, to shear. To lister: to furrow the land—plow and drill—drop and cover. Who is the one that compiles? Roll clouds scroll the sky. Call it and we will listen: anything but *there is no list, there is no list.*

4. CATECHISM

What is the chief end of human life?

Sirens like a trumpet's call.
Roll the beds to the hall
and pull the blinds—too late—

What reason have you for saying so?

Burst rose of sharded light.
IV lines ripped loose, beds thrown
against the wall, blood-drenched

What is the highest good of man?

and bathed in life. And these
are the lucky ones, the blessed
who walk among our ruin.

*What is, what reason, what is
the good of man?*

The very same. Bathed in life,
the burst rose. O sharded
light, sirens like a trumpet's call.

5. BROKEN

Stripped and strafed—another
casualty—their skeletons

spear the sky. Shag-barked
hickory, catalpa, a 135-ringed oak.

Debris perches like turkey
vultures on their arms.

Each one, a splintered body
to be hewn and dragged out

of town, put to the pyre.
They deserve this much, at least.

Smoke masses, and
grief re-greens the sky.

puncture wound   hard black
center   —press—
let the pain remind you
what it means   to survive
decay   a petri dish   leaf
mold and wood   what the skin
admits   all nature needs
to destroy you   *Spore*
fr. *spora*   sowing seed

I will see your toll   and raise you
one hundred sixty-one

7. DOVECOTE

windows blown-in
and empty-socketed as a skull
against the hospital's
bone-slabbed concrete—

roost, thou forsaken

—absence is its own home

Lance and drain this ravened sky—hat in hand we will
Always return to you, prodigal. I swear we knew
Not what we did. I swear. Land unscrubbed to rust,
Gashed and bare—hell's toothed pastoral. No
Excuses. Pitchfork my soul, millet on your scale, but
Let not this harvest strip flesh from bones. Pray
Unsheathe your sword and make of my heart a ragged tear.
Salvage this earth, snarl grass and field. I will take it all.

BLACK HORIZON

Grand Isle, Louisiana, 2010
Post-Deepwater Horizon oil spill

Like ribbons of kelp, they wash up
bark-black and stretching
far as the eye can see—boys
sway in the waves, skin sheened
in oil as they toss the tar balls.
A quick game of pickup.
On the shore, cleanup crews
weave a path between beach
towels, Hazmat-suited,
shovel and plastic bag in hand.
It never fails to shock: dark
pools oiling sands of blinding
white. I load my open palms
with them, testing their heft.
These scales cannot be balanced.
And always more cresting
the waves, merciful as death.

IN WHICH SHE OPENS THE BOX

Celia Steele in Delaware, 1923

1.

Even as a child I hungered
        for them, fox in the henhouse,

my mother said. And a whole lot
        worse. When I opened the box

to 500 straw-padded eggs instead
        of the 50 I ordered, I wasn't

thinking waste not, want not
        or, a chicken in every pot.

I was thinking how I'd grown.
        Thinking of life, and how

can anyone argue with that?
        The yolk's yellow chalk afloat

in its wet ether. A world unto
        itself—the only thing on which

my mother and I ever
        agreed. I don't blame her.

I was the one who palmed
        the family's last egg and peeled

its shell free: a flurry of white
       to be buried in the dirt

out back like bones. I couldn't
       confess, not even when she'd

looped and hung the dish towel
       like a noose about my neck, stool

wobbling beneath my feet.
       When I saw those 500 neat-

packed eggs on my doorstep, it
       was her sour-milk cloth I felt

beneath my chin. The same
       bald want. I saw no harm

in it, in desiring that ocher sun's
       crumble upon the tongue.

2.

I thought I knew about cages, about the boxes
we are born to, rows of eggs nestled in a crate.
I thought I knew about the cruelty of men.
I knew a lot of things: the clipped mouth, the feet
bound, "the dark night of the soul." A life
doled out, grain by grain. Woman's flesh-bound
bones: meat to be consumed. Suffering
a sun-cured body, powdered feather-bronze.
I never thought *men* could mean me, never
imagined lives of literal night. I thought
I knew cages, knew boxes. Thought man
could invent nothing worse than what I knew.

ELEGY, SUNG IN DIRT

after the New York Times *image of the*
Deepwater Horizon's collapse into the sea

Feather-vaned, the smoke
    flows up, black-

blooded as the oil plumes
    that will soon unwind

below. Boats spray
    forth arcs of salted

water, suspended
    by the camera's shutter.

Before evening
    this image—viral elegy—

will echo across screen and page.
    I cannot look. No,

I am the poet of the eye
    filled with dirt. Mouth

shut. But tell me
    who among you could conjure

the gift, at such depths,
    of seeing in the dark?

MUD

The italicized text is taken from an interview
with Keith Jones, father of Gordon Jones,
a victim of the Deepwater Horizon explosion

Because that's what it looks like.
Because we don't know what it is,
not exactly. Cocktail of clay,
chemicals, heavy minerals—

the companies aren't saying. For
the Macondo well, the drilling
mud ran BP ~$10 million.

To "cork the pipe" is to displace
mud with seawater—it's worth
too much to leave behind—
and siphon it to a ship standing by.

But the mud was disappearing
down the hole. When a well
loses mud, it means nothing good.

It kicks. Underground
formation: unstable.
@ 9:44 p.m., from the drill shack:
"We have mud going to the crown."

I know what my fervent prayer is.
It's that Gordon never felt it. But I know
who Gordon was and that he knew

when stuff is gushing out of the well head . . .
@ 9:45, "The well is blown out."
First the mud and then the cement.
Soot rain from the derrick.

Earth's exhale: a match's lit hiss.
He knew that the worst is about to happen.
Gordon knew what a blowout was.
Everybody does.

FIELD NOTE, 2011

for Wilbert Collins,
Golden Meadow, Louisiana

I raise my camera, spinning
its iris. Focus shuttered and caught.
Not a glyph hollowed out, but
a voice written in light.

Collins Oyster Co.
Out of Business After 90 Yrs.
Because of BP's Oil and
Governor Jindal's Fresh Water

Sweat darkens my shirt,
shape of a hand pressing.
To my right, Route 1's traffic hurtles
past. "Ninety years!" a man

shouts, and idles his car.
Points to the sign. "My father's
out back. Go talk to him."

ET IN ARCADIA EGO

Nicolas Poussin, 1637–38

I too
      was in Arcadia—sudden

granite tomb risen
      from the planet's pasture.

But mourning is no
      great riddle. All is fated

to extinction: this
      afternoon walk, a countryside

soon to be ravaged by war,
      an infant heavy

on his mother's chest, stone
      head in churned earth.

SUBURBAN ELEGY

In 2010, the prevalence of household food insecurity in suburban areas was 12.6 percent (6.2 million households).

US DEPARTMENT OF AGRICULTURE

The paved street on which they live
has sent out roots,
        tarred black, to split

cul de sac and yard. Of Famine,
Ovid wrote: her parchment
        skin revealed the bowels

within; her sagging breasts
seemed hardly fastened to her ribs.
        A woman steers her cart

down ALDI's aisles, calculator
in hand. Red kidney
        beans, $1.25/lb.

Her son's lips crust white,
and in her sleep she sees her infant
        girl's throat, scaly

with scurf. Milk: two for $4.
The numbers run over.
        She returns the cylinder

of juice to its shelf, suffers
the small metal click.

FIELD NOTE, 2011

for Wilbert Collins, Golden Meadow, Louisiana

"The fresh water was as bad
as the oil," Collins says of attempts
to force oil from the marshes.

His dining room turned war-
room, three card tables pushed
together and a wall papered

floor to ceiling in maps: Jefferson Parish's
oyster lease-lines, the Collins beds
thumb-tacked red.

Report: *more than 60% of oysters*
in one Louisiana bay are dead as a result
of the release of freshwater.

He will reseed the beds this year.
In fifteen more, maybe, the oysters
will be back. I nod, pivoting.

Then stop. Opposite the charts
hangs a photo, pre-spill:
Collins on the *Braud and Tragy's*

deck, head tipped to the sky.
"A typical haul," he tells me.
I zoom in, filling the viewfinder.

That day's dredge of mollusks
—I never imagined so many—
heaped in piles higher than his knees.

from the required predrilling threat analysis,
submitted by BP to the Department of the
Interior's Mineral Management Service,
February 2009

Worst Case Scenario Determination: volume, uncontrolled
blowout per day: 162,000 gallons of crude oil; a discussion of
response to an oil spill resulting from the activities proposed in
this plan is not required; a site-specific Oil Spill Response Plan
is not required

It is unlikely that an accidental spill would occur from the
proposed activities.

~

Threatened or Endangered Species: 29 species of marine mammals
reside in the Gulf of Mexico. There are 28 species of cretacea
and 1 sirenian species, the manatee. Five [species of] sea turtles
inhabit the Gulf of Mexico and are listed as Endangered.
The Leatherback, Green, Hawksbill, Kemp's Ridley, and
Loggerback turtle. Five baleen whales, one toothed whale,
and one sirenian exist in the Gulf of Mexico and are listed
Endangered under the Endangered Species Act: the Northern
Right Whale, the Blue Whale, the Fin Whale, the Sei Whale,
the Humpback Whale, the Sperm Whale, the West Indian
Manatee

A discussion of the measures that would be taken to avoid,
minimize, and mitigate impacts to the marine and coastal

environments and habitats, biota, and threatened and endangered species is not required.

~

birds could become oiled

~

Beaches: due to the distance from shore (48 miles) and the response capabilities that would be implemented, no significant adverse impacts are anticipated; *Wetlands:* due to the distance from shore (48 miles) and the response capabilities that would be implemented, no significant adverse impacts are anticipated; *Shore Birds and Coastal Nesting Birds*: due to the distance from shore (48 miles) and the response capabilities that would be implemented, no significant adverse impacts are anticipated; *Coastal Wildlife Refuges*: due to the distance from shore (48 miles) and the response capabilities that would be implemented, no significant adverse impacts are anticipated; *Wilderness Areas*: due to the distance from shore (48 miles) and the response capabilities that would be implemented, no significant adverse impacts are anticipated

~

no adverse effects to fisheries are anticipated

~

few lethal effects are expected from oil spills; oil spills and oil spill response activities could cause declines in [sea turtle] survival or productivity, resulting in gradual population declines

27

No adverse impacts to threatened or endangered sea turtles are anticipated.

~

No agencies or persons were consulted regarding potential impacts associated with the proposed activities.

"I hereby certify that BP Exploration & Production, Inc. has the capability to respond, to the maximum extent practicable, to a worst-case discharge."

BLOWOUT

*from the testimony of survivors Micah
Sandell, Steve Bertone, Douglas Brown,
and Randy Ezell, as recorded in the National
Commission on the BP Deepwater Horizon
Oil Spill and Offshore Drilling's Report to
the President*

up on the main deck   I seen mud
shooting all the way up to the derrick   gas
and smoke filled   so loud   like taking an air
hose and sticking it in your ear   starboard
explosion   knocked to the floor   —fire—
to the back of the cab   hands on my head

          *

a freight train thumping in my head
lights out   a man so coated in blood
I had no idea who   PA System: *Fire.*
Fire. Fire.   taste and smell of fuel   gas
fire from derrick leg to leg out the starboard
window   "they're all gone"   methane air

          *

in the engine control room   loud air
leak sound   the alarms wailed and I heard
well-control situation   fell through subfloor
amid cable trays   wires   into the mud-
dark   buried under ceiling   gas
ripping   engine rev   a second blast fired

*

look down   in the moon pool only fire's
solid sheet   look up   nothing here
but flames way past the crown   deck gassed
slick   one and a half inches deep   —head
for the lifeboats   abandon ship—   mud
thick as mucus   "don't slip"   starboard

*

heat and smoke erupting from the rig   sun-star
bright   a blast furnace   the fire
our only light   I crawled over rubble
over a body   I could feel the droplets of air
misting my skin   methane   heard
an ocean on fire   a deafening roar of lit gas

*

"have we EDSed"   *"yes"*   "have we EDSed,
I have to be certain"   *"yes"*   the control board
lit red   debris-clogged ether   the jumpers' heads
visible amid the waves   and on fire-
licked rafts the passengers suspended in air
"we need a knife"   terror's coat   a dense mud

*

on the *Bankston* a black torrent   *(head back*
500 m.)   an egret mud-covered on starboard deck
and that pyre   the dead the very air we breathe

TO WALK ON AIR

for Mike Williams,
the last man to jump off the rig

Columns of flame and smoke uncoil
    reptilian in the night,
rubbing against the rig's sides.
    Across crest and trough,
the serpent feeds on the fuel pooled
    below— *We're going to burn up.*
Or we're going to jump. And they
    drop straight through its bodied heat,
feet cycling air. Their boots
    pierce cloud as they crash
into a sea stirred to wildfire.
    A hand reaches out, gathering
them in, as the rig boils black
    and then curls back upon itself.

ELEGY FOR THE ELEVEN

1. SHEILA CLARK, OVER TEA

for Donald Clark

It was right here he came to me,
on the porch, overlooking
these soybean fields gone to
nothing. First the land, then the sea.

It was always the wrong place
at the wrong time for him—
we didn't talk about it—
but where else is a man to turn.

At first I thought it was
the loblolly's shadow hung across
the porch, snapping like wash
pinned to the line. That fast,

the wind brought him in.
Here's the thing: when a man
comes visiting, he spreads his wings
dark as a bat's, soft-furred and hot

as all those nights, no breeze,
just his skin on mine. I should've
known. Love can turn a man
to flame. Not that he said

anything, I'm not crazy,
but when the sun split
him wide, he left me this, look,
my body veined in soot.

2. PUMP ROOM

for Shane Roshto, Adam Weise, Roy Kemp

If earth is a blue balloon, is kelp
bladder, then the drill's bit is a pin pushed
as far as it can go, until—everything

that could go wrong was going
wrong. He'd call before and after
every shift. I think the earth is

telling us she just doesn't want
to be drilled here, he said. The well
from hell, he said. The drill's bit

pulling slurry to the pit for them
to disjoin and send back down as far
as it could go until everything

just went. They were the second
to go. Like a balloon, it doesn't take
much, as every child knows, until
the pin will break skin. Will explode.

for Aaron Dale Burkeen, crane operator

Metaphor is power, don't kid yourself,
the writer says. It cannot be divorced
from ethos. The crane's stake
not licked but engulfed in fire's craw.
He made it halfway down the ladder.
Precision. No, the other writer says,
it is the job of poetry to feed
empathy, and the end justifies any means.
When we scattered my aunt's ashes
off the Monhegan breakwater, my cousin
wouldn't look—she knew how
the body persists: bone and tooth
crowned gold, splinted relics amid downy
ash. I shift in my seat. Eyes on me. Yes,
show them that man pitched like a child's
doll, slammed to the floor in a fit
of temper. You misunderstand the nature
of likenesses. Willfully, the writer says.
An academic's argument. No, simile
can incinerate a man as surely as death
can disappear him, a fireball
splitting starboard deck. But how else
to bring it home, a listener asks.
There must be some way to say this.

4. THE MUD ROOM

for Gordon Jones, Blair Manuel, Karl Kleppinger

They were the first
         to go. Mud and gas
rising, two and a half
         miles of earth
and another mile of sea.
         Some depths aren't
meant to be plumbed.
         I am no believer,
but still I pray—let
         their souls shake off
this planet's weight like
         a dog fresh
from the bath, let them
         open, speckled
stargazer lilies from well-
         soaked soil, and let
that perfume wrap
         their loved ones
in comfort, sun-warmed
         stole on rasped skin.
This is what I should say.
         But in June, the hole
still spilling itself into
         the Gulf, as lilies
startle my garden pink
         and gold, I put faith
in what I know best.
         Hate—after all
these years, you owe me
         this much, at least—

let the oilmen drown
      at their desks,
grind them bitumen black
      as snuffed wicks. Let
them expire beneath
      the pewtered bell,
its terrible weight.

for Dewey Revette, Stephen Curtis, Jason Anderson

No one knows what happened. The rig is not saying. The well stretched farther down than Mt. Everest is up. Jason said, "I've got this," the displacement test read negative. All around, that night, the moon sparked jellyfish in waves of fire. They call the driller's shack the doghouse, the core of the ship, the rope between the heart and the mind. What we do know: there should have been sirens, lights flashing, operations shut down. But there was only silence. A blue screen of death. *The damn thing's been on bypass for five years*, the subsea supervisor said. *Just like the entire fleet.* Gas wound round the rig like a mangrove snake before it strikes. *Who wants to wake up at 3 a.m. for a false alarm?* The company man said with his eyes: say nothing. At 9:41, the blowout preventer failed and the rig stayed joined. We have nothing more to report. The Horizon lost to lower midnight, benthic, the ocean like a winding sheet. Its throat stuffed shut with the testimony of the dead, black-carapaced and clicking.

DAYBREAK

Percussive, the migraine   Shoots tender
—bile-green—   Untying their leaves

This is the fallout   The expert says
This is what happens   Neuritis: disarray: disunion

The body's nave   Will drive its point home
(even if we won't hear it)   Will drive it back

Underground—   It tunnels, deliberate
Like the star mole   His diamond-bit mouth

We black it all out   Call counterfeit on
A throb of feather-drift   Our eyes, our skin

This is the linchpin   Leaking, spleen-pitched

THERE LIES THE HYDRA

BP and the Obama administration attacked
the monster with chemical dispersants . . .
only to have it break up into hundreds of
millions of smaller, more terrible parts.

—ANTONIA JUHASZ, BLACK TIDE

1. HERACLES AND THE HYDRA

Attic red, the serpent's figure
        rises out of abyssal black,
thick-bodied, its brute
        column flanked by our hero
and his love. Long odds,
        this, mere scythe and torch
to the winding water-snake's
        poison breath and twelve

branching heads. Cut one
        and two more take its place—
oh fruitful wound, this
        house that feeds on death,
that multiplies doom.

2. COREXIT 9527A

:: to scatter the singular
gall to a manifold might

:: to disperse, to split
and suspend, to glitter fierce
in loose veils of oil

:: Statius—*sunken, there lies*
the Hydra. and cunning
grows dark in death agony.

:: sorbitan; propanediol;
ethanol; butoxy– .
sodium salt (1:1); octa-
decenoate. distillates;
petroleum; hydrotreated
light

:: to masticate dive gear,
boat engines, citizens' skin

:: pockets of orange
and pink like a sun settling
over the sea floor

3. BOOM AND SKIM

Vermiform, the citrus-bright
barriers float, shoring up
sheens of oil for the boomers
to vacuum and scoop, to bar

access to land. The crude
slick slips their Styrofoam
grip, even as authorities
outfit trawlers with more boom

to net oil instead of oyster,
shrimp, or crab. The Macondo
glitters, mirror-city teeming
as the Hydra's flexed scales,

water's dark-blue steel
embossed both silver and gold.

TO NARCISSUS

1. NARCISSUS ADDRESSES HIS BELOVED

Chest matching each crest
and trough of my own,
you breathe: viscid beauty
pooling the ravine's rust-

needled floor. Let love rip
across your visage and gloss
its skin—my heart's bell
flares gold, valved muscle

an open chamber, yes,
—thirst chokes the throat—
lie with me here, ringed in
distant pickets of tree. My love,

we constitute the garden.

2. TO NARCISSUS *(VERB)*:

to stir up, to trawl, to gratify
one's self—

"I know it when I see it"

the sea a tarred slurry,
"the gaff between the fisher's hand
and the creature's eye . . ."

to master, to
spill, to trickle down,

to runoff, to top kill, to fire
the gene gun
             a sterile organism

"safe as table salt"

to lagoon in waste, to defile
and demand, to screw—

BACKYARD PASTORAL

In her backyard, weeds proliferate,
        bald dandelions, flocks
of garlic mustard, thistle. She straps

        her son into his infant carrier,
face to her chest, and drapes
        a thin blanket over his head.

To protect him from the sun.
        Used according to directions, Roundup
poses no risk to people, animals,

        or the environment. Just
Pump-n-Go: she starts in the backyard.
        Got to get it done before

it rains, before tomorrow's
        playdate. *Leaves no residue.*
Mist hits her nose and lungs,

        and she coughs. One palm burns.
In the news: *men exposed more than*
        two days a year had twice the risk

of lymphoma. Her son stirs. She pats
        his back and keeps going. Later,
she'll read: *Roundup can be the origin*

        of a cancer that will develop
30 or 40 years later. She closes her eyes
        and folds the newspaper shut.

IN WHICH SHE CONSIDERS THE WATER

Flint, Michigan, 2016

The river rushes and beats her
    home. Through phosphate-scaled
plumbing, it veins the walls' plaster
    skin and water bleeds
orange chloride from the tap. The pipes
    leach. The lead—*no*
imminent threat to public health—seeps
    and floats like a ghost, silent,
straight from the Flint to her child's
plastic cup. Lead levels peak
    at 13,200 ppb and the pipes moan:
what was done cannot be
    undone. Fill a glass. Hold it
to the light. No one here to see.

ELEGY, A CATALOGUE

The Arctic puddles to soot   asphalt black
     Its albedo: to zero

Bufo periglenes   seven golden bodies enamel-
     bright (last seen May 15, 1989)

Coal dust clouds my eyes   blackout
     curtains that refuse the migraine light

The disaster is related to forgetfulness   debris
     drifts   *forgetfulness without memory*

And more new terms for this new earth
     functionally extinct extreme climate

refugees   a season of forest-fed smoke
     a life ringed in fog

Gone: red-bellied gracile opossum   bluebuck
     Columbian grebe   A rip for-

ever ripping   To "How worried should we be?"
     I ask, "How lucky do you feel?"

Inupiat for ice: *sikuliaq*, young ice   *sarri*,
     pack ice   *tuvaq*, landlocked ice   No word

for this jigsawed melt   Jackhammer to floe

Newton's parakeet   desert rat-kangaroo
     Hawkins' rail   olive ibis   the vaquita

Louisiana's Isle de Jean Charles   all rust and mildew
        and the Houma   land drowning in salt

Methane rising out of the Strodhalen mire

No one knows how much carbon
        nests there suspended, waiting

for the match   Or how to put it out
        Schlegel: *Every poet is Narcissus*

Polar vortex   Permafrost sickle bearing down
        The threshold   the heat of darkness

Queen of Sheba's gazelle   Baiji dolphin
        New Zealand quail   coral reefs bleached

To recall is to re-member, to re-collect   Is the voice
        repeating always the self-same thing

The toddler's endless echo of the last word spoken
        The exact blue scent of childhood's snow

Tragedy, an accident recounted in lacunae
        gaps   tears   and other interruptions

On the IUCN Red List: white ferula mushroom
        European ground squirrel   silver

thistle   This is vespers   this the bell
        the only vessel

What could one more matter

The experience of the sixth great extinction
       of disaster   is the one we all live

without purpose   All we have is yearning and

Its zenith, zero hour

FIELD NOTE, 2011

for Wilbert Collins, Golden Meadow, Louisiana

He poses for me, now-empty
deck behind him, arm braced
on a stanchion. Both eyes sink
into his cap's angled shadows.
At his feet, the split shells
of last year opalesce, a hollowed
light. "I don't have anything
else to do," he says,
when I thank him. "I offered
to show them all my dead oysters.
They don't want to see it."
I know. It's not in our nature.
I owe him more than this
utterance unheard—
must learn, at last, to look.

I steer the rental car down a road that doesn't appear on any
map. Bayous cut a brown-edged lace around me, once-lush
green fields matted and manged. Count the casualties: sargas-
sum and spartina grass, bald cypress, tupelo gum, wax myrtles
and black mangroves. Thick beds of seagrass.

~

As if by an artist's crude
massed strokes, the pelican's
beak is daub, is plaster.
She rises from the bay's water,
limbs out and hung in tatters
of oil—our angel, wings
heavy and mouth cast open
always. She is scarved
blind and deaf. Tarped mute.

~

Lignite, lime, and shale;
          salt-sheeted; sanded
stone. *No, no, go not to—*
          Barataria Bay
like a broad, marled bowl.

~

The biologist's rule of thumb:
at least ten dead for every one found.

By August, more than 2,000
oil-soaked pelicans had been picked up
dead or dying. Another
1,200 were found dead after eating
fish contaminated by oil.

Cleanup workers report:
We throw them back. If we kept
all the dead fish and birds,
we'd have mountains of both.
We throw them back.

~

Tiger Pass Seafood, Louisiana

Daniel Moreau and his men idle on deck, stitching net. Boats
can't afford to go out, he explains. Gas costs. No white shrimp
this year, just balls of oil. *We've seen bad seasons and we've pulled it
out. We can't pull it out this time.* He offers me a satsuma, to stay
for lunch. The two men left working for him now share a room
above the office. *Do you feel forgotten?* I ask. *A good person helps
people*, he says. Adjusts the visor on his cap.

~

Helicoptered to Fort Jackson,
starved keen, the bird
smothered within her own
feathered skin. Washed in Dawn,
they IV'd then released her
back to a sea smeared
the color of mud, of old blood.

~

The dirt road ends. I lower my window. In the distance, a truck's engine. Then nothing: I can't hear the bugs; I don't see the birds.

A HIVE OF BOXES

Document:
1. Teaching; a piece of instruction, a lesson; a warning
2. Evidence, proof
3. Something written, inscribed, engraved, etc., which provides evidence or information or serves as a record

~

My car idles on the road's shoulder. Outside, the Louisiana air steams. I let the open window wash out the car's false chill. Looking around, I pull my notebook from the glove box and press pen to paper.

If I held a mirror to this place, could its breath still blossom the glass?

~

Deepwater Horizon

A fifth-generation semi-submersible rig, the Deepwater Horizon was a bit like an aircraft carrier with a derrick on the deck instead of an airport. It wasn't anchored over the drill site; it floated on massive pontoons dipping seventy-six feet into the sea. Tethered to the well by a thread of steel pipe twenty-one inches wide, the rig was held in place by what's called dynamic positioning, a sophisticated computer-controlled system that operated eight giant thrusters, 7,375 horsepower apiece, to keep the rig centered over the well. . . . Six diesel engines with a combined force of sixty thousand horsepower drove generators that kicked out forty-two thousand kilowatts,

enough electricity to light a good-sized town. It had a deck
the size of two football fields and a derrick twenty-four stories
high.

—Peter Lehner

~

I spend hours scrolling through news articles about the
Macondo blowout. Images of wildlife coated in oil. Phrases:
British Petroleum. Eleven dead. Largest accidental oil spill. But
reading isn't enough; I've lived decades in books and know how
soon the articles will drop off the front page, then disappear
completely.

The only thing worse than the disaster itself is what happens
when the world decides it's over. All fixed. It's a fact any
survivor knows.

Who will witness what follows danger's first aftermath?
Who will document the crisis that bleeds on and on?

~

Et in Arcadia Ego
Nicolas Poussin, 1650, oil on canvas

In the center of Poussin's painting, a tombstone interrupts
verdant Arcadia. Brute awakening, in such a rural paradise,
this first encounter with death. Four shepherds face the stone.
On the left, a man sinks into melancholy; another kneels and
dares to touch the words chiseled there. A single woman
stands, staring down this mortal end. I am the one on the right,
pointing, asking anyone anywhere to make sense of what this
could mean.

~

"Modern ecopoetry refuses the more conventional forms of cultural absorption in which past ways of life are destroyed, then idealized and transferred to an imaginary space. It sustains the sense of emergency. In doing this, however, modern ecopoetry also creates a more straightforward anticipatory mourning."

—*Bonnie Costello*

In other words: The poet grieves not only a particular death, a particular extinction. She mourns the death of nature itself, as if it has already come to pass.

~

At home, it possesses and drives me, live spillcam as compulsion, and I watch the well bleed.

~

Our windowless classroom is a box, buried in Curtin Hall's basement. I am teaching a seminar on the elegy. I read "Meditation at Lagunitas" aloud and repeat the line: "A word is elegy to what it signifies."

We listen to the lights hum. Silence stretches me on its rack. The seconds are hours and the clock's hands black as a tar mat. Black as smoke coughed up by oil burns. I skim my fingers over the desk, train of thought dispersing.

~

> "Cold Pastoral!
> When old age shall this generation waste,
>   Thou shalt remain, in midst of other woe . . ."
>
> —John Keats

~

DAYBREAK

Harnessed and sun-spurred,
another day slices the blinds.

Her night's sleep rumpled
as lake water by a surfacing head—

morning drills her, a migraine
splintered black and light.

There is no song to sing.
Only the kick in her sides—

too late to draw the sheet back
over her eyes. Now she opens

her lungs wide, admits
remembering's wet-gray pour.

~

Each man described this strange transparent fluid moving
across the drill deck. That fluid was gas. When the gas reached
the mud pits . . . they were the first to die, that's where the
first explosion happened. Now the gas continued to ignite
back to the drill floor. The second explosion was the drill floor,

that's where those people got incinerated instantly. . . . It was
that damn gas that got loose. That's the killer. Once that fire
happened and then they couldn't get loose from the well, that's
when the Deepwater Horizon becomes toast.

—*Professor Robert Bea*

~

Narcissus is to man as Echo is to poetry.

"Echoes are literally how poetry, as sheer writing or as
sheer voice, carries on after our own, or the Poet's, or the
protagonist's, voice has died away. They are the earth of
poetry, the weeds of writing growing up out of the cracks of
significance."

—*Timothy Morton*

~

from SUMMER WALK

Milkwort and rampion writhe
in the Dolomite promontories'
cragged and shark-tooth jaw.
Snagged in their occluded grip,
the companions walk with care: cast
to melancholy, they cannot bear
to crush any life that has fought
rocky crack and split to light . . .

They refuse to listen, to hear
how the word *heaven* lingers, holds
the echo of its end—

~

The Ekphrastic Endeavor

Pixelated, the image *L'Angelus* by Jean-François Millet fills my
computer screen. Zoom in. I recall the Dalí painting: another
couple, in another barren landscape. *Such stillness is its own
death.* But the moment expands until the painting breathes,
until it occupies the inhalation before the woman releases her
keen, before the man will drop his hand to her shoulder. It is
the moment before the lament.

I step inside the picture's space and time, its vibrant web.
I stand outside the image, in my own space and time. All
the same moment. The ekphrastic moment an elegy to the
singular self.

~

They think hiding the oil on the bottom will fix the problem.
It won't. Water is continuous. What is on the bottom has to
come up. The Gulf current is strong. We have to worry about
this not just today and tomorrow, but for future years.
                  —*James Billiot, fisherman, to reporter Antonia Juhasz*

~

I do nothing by half-measures and my mind is tired of its hive
of boxes.

~

Et in Arcadia Ego

As Erwin Panofsky pointed out in a classic essay on the Poussin painting, the phrase is understood less in its medieval sense— where Death is the speaker and the image is a warning in the present tense: And I, Death, am even in Arcadia—than in a Virgilian and post-Renaissance sense, where the voice seems to be that of the deceased and speaks in the past tense: I also (like you) once lived in Arcady.

          —*Elizabeth Helsinger*

~

Before, my poems were filled with lines like these:

> *I finally see how my life must always be . . .*
> *there is / no difference between the living / and the dead . . .*
> *threading and rethreading / the legs with transparent ties . . .*

Before, my poems were caged, boxed, locked away.

> *(Robert Motherwell:* Before, my work had been personal
> and intimate, and even though the first version was
> a very small picture and a wholly unexpected one, I
> realized that what was different about it was that it was
> basically a monumental, public image.)

Now, I fear that the air I breathe will flee, even as I continue in a world that disappears around me. I fear closure, the sharp click of thought like my jewelry box's snap as it shuts.

I try so hard to wake. To glean what remains of this harvest. To wipe the webs free.

as though the spirit might
aspire, in its last act,
to walk on air.

—*Amy Clampitt*

~

Please Leave

1. BP Claims Office: Camera slung over one shoulder, I enter. A woman asks what I need it for. "Pictures," I say, holding the camera's black box with both hands. Not permitted, I'm told.

2. Refinery: It stretches for over a mile on the left side of the road. The smokestacks exhale carbon-black fumes and I stop the car to climb out and take a picture. Before I can get back in, the police car pulls up behind me. He asks if I have permission.

"I need your license," he says. Takes it and returns to his car.

I wait. Sit down in the driver's seat, door ajar. Stand back up.

"I'm not going to take the camera," he says. "Not this time."

"Thanks," I say. Then, "Why do the police patrol here?"

"We don't," he says. Hooks fingers in belt loops. Looks away. Shrugs.

~

The modern elegist tends not to achieve but to resist consolation, not to override but to sustain anger, not to heal but to reopen the wounds of loss.

—*Jahan Ramazani*

~

If you wander the beach, it's still littered with tar balls, even this long after. Kids build castles, bodysurf the waves. On the radio, an ad sponsored by BP urges people back to the beaches, reminds them of shrimp and jambalaya, and encourages them to come see. Dead fish mark the high tide line, most of the beach fenced off, still not clean.

I ask a trawler if he eats what he catches. Not the tar, he half-jokes, dodging the question. I ask again and he admits he doesn't. Not anymore.

~

Yet I'm not dreaming. I look into your eyes . . . and I see only kindness, human-kindness. Calm down, I tell myself, you are making a mountain out of a molehill. This is life. Everyone else comes to terms with it, why can't you? Why can't you?

—*J. M. Coetzee*

~

An egg cracked into a cut-glass bowl. Clear
sky, a single cloud, and the floating sun.

Its white God-throat like a wolf's howl.
Its long patience, needled teeth, at her heels.

How Apollo hauled this ball of rags, tallow-
soaked, from the baleen sea's blue hour.

A torch, a pendant, a burning wheel.
Eyelids steamed open like a mollusk's shell.

Like the light they shine in a dead man's eye,
this perfect black pool. And the ink spreading.

ACKNOWLEDGMENTS

Cutthroat, A Journal of the Arts: "Elegy for the Eleven"
Hawai'i Pacific Review: "Narcissus in Paradise"
The Journal: "Elegy Written in Oil"
Kenyon Review Online: "Blowout"
Mobius: "Elegy, a Catalogue" (as "Still Life")
New Mexico Review: "Atavism at Twilight," "Elegy Sung in Dirt,"
    "Black Horizon," "There Lies the Hydra"
The Rumpus: "Mnemosyne to the Poet"
Terrain.org: "Elegy, Wind-Whipped" (as "Morning: Joplin, MO")
Vandal: "Backyard Pastoral" (as part of "Transgenic Pastoral")
Verse Wisconsin: "Celia Steele Opens the Box" (as "The Modern
    Hen") and "Field Note 1, 2, and 3," (as "Fresh Water")
West Branch: "Summer Walk"

"Elegy, Wind-Whipped" was awarded first prize in *Terrain.org*'s
annual poetry contest.

"Elegy for the Eleven" was awarded second prize in *Cutthroat*'s 2011
Joy Harjo Poetry Contest.

This book was made possible by the University of Wisconsin-Milwau-
kee's Research Growth Initiative program and its Center for 21st Cen-
tury Studies, as well as fellowships from the Sustainable Arts Founda-
tion and the Vermont Studio Center's James Merrill Fellowship. I am
grateful for all of your generosity.

A special thanks to Daniel Slager for his faith in this book, and to Joy Katz for her phenomenal editorial guidance. Thanks also to all of the people who make Milkweed Editions such an amazing press and without whom this book wouldn't exist. For inspiration and advice, I also want to thank Brittany Cavallaro, Aviva Cristy, Steve Gehrke, Rebecca Hazelton, Cynthia Hoffman, Jesse Lee Kercheval, Jacqueline Kolosov, Eric Pankey, Nancy Reddy, Rita Mae Reese, and Angela Voras-Hills, as well as the graduate students in my Fall 2013 manuscript workshop.

Most of all, I want to thank my children, Simon and Anna, for their patient support, and my husband, Mark Pioli, for his incisive feedback and unwavering belief in both me and this project. You are my rock.

REBECCA DUNHAM is the author of three previous books of poetry: *Glass Armonica*, winner of the Lindquist & Vennum Prize for Poetry; *The Flight Cage*; and *The Miniature Room*, winner of the T. S. Eliot Prize. She has been the recipient of an NEA Fellowship and was the 2005–6 Jay C. and Ruth Halls Fellow in Poetry at the Wisconsin Institute for Creative Writing. She is a professor of English at the University of Wisconsin-Milwaukee and lives in Madison, Wisconsin.

Interior design by Gretchen Achilles/Wavetrap Design
Typeset in Dante
by Gretchen Achilles/Wavetrap Design

Dante was designed shortly after World War II by Giovanni Mardersteig, the Italian printer and founder of Officina Bodoni. It was later redrawn and adapted by Monotype in 1957. It is an old-style serif font known for the graceful harmony between its roman and italic characters.